Fact Finders®

PEOPLE YOU SHOULD KNOW

STEVEN SPIELBERG

Get to Know the Extraordinary Filmmaker

by Judy Greenspan

Consultant: Stuart Weinstock
Columbia University

CAPSTONE PRESS
a capstone imprint

Fact Finders Books are published by Capstone Press, an imprint of Capstone.
1710 Roe Crest Drive, North Mankato, Minnesota 56003
www.capstonepub.com

Library of Congress Cataloging-in-Publication Data is available on the Library of Congress website.
ISBN 978-1-5435-9108-8 (library binding)
ISBN 978-1-4966-6581-2 (paperback)
ISBN 978-1-5435-9109-5 (eBook PDF)

Summary: Steven Spielberg has changed the cinematic world with his hugely popular films. Testing out new technology, telling dramatic stories, and collaborating with successful directors, actors, and producers helped build Spielberg's reputation as a director and producer.

Photo Credits
Alamy: AF Archive, 7, 23, The Hollywood Archive/PictureLux, 8; Getty Images: Fotos International/Universal Pictures, cover; Newscom: Album/Columbia Pictures, 12, 16, Digital Press Photos/Beitia Archives, 24, Glasshouse Images, 5, United Archives/IFTN, 19, United Archives/Impress, 20, Zuma Press/Michael Jacobs, 11; Shutterstock: Featureflash Photo Agency, 27, 28, pablopicasso, 14

Design Elements by Shutterstock

Editorial Credits
Mari Bolte, editor; Dina Her, designer; Svetlana Zhurkin, media researcher;
Tori Abraham, production specialist

Source Notes
page 6, line 11: Chris Nashawaty. "Steven Spielberg Talks About 'Jaws'—The Greatest Summer Movie Ever Made." https://ew.com/article/2011/06/08/steven-spielberg-jaws-interview/. Accessed May 11, 2019.

page 8, line 3: Susan Lacy, director. Spielberg. 2017.

page 9, line 7: ibid.

page 9, sidebar, line 2: Jon Burlingame. "John Williams Recalls Jaws." http://www.filmmusicsociety.org/news_events/features/2012/081412.html. Accessed June 1, 2019.

page 8, sidebar, line 7: Jeff Lunden. "John Williams' Inevitable Themes." https://www.npr.org/sections/deceptivecadence/2012/11/10/164615420/john-williams-inevitable-themes. Accessed June 11, 2019.

page 12, line 5: Spielberg.

page 13, line 11: Joseph McBride. Steven Spielberg: A Biography. New York: Da Capo Press, 1999, page 12.

page 20, line 2: Spielberg.

page 20, line 6: McBride, page 328.

page 21, line 1: Retrocade Podcast. The Making of E.T. the Extra-Terrestrial. https://www.youtube.com/watch?v=pHsCTJOdNjk. Accessed June 10, 2019.

page 22, line 16: Spielberg.

page 23, line 18: Sara Debbie Gutfreund. "Steven Spielberg's Jewish Roots." https://www.aish.com/jw/s/Steven-Spielbergs-Jewish-Roots.html#.WI43_04yMqk. mailto. Accessed June 10, 2019.

page 25, line 7: Ian Freer. "Steven Spielberg and Special Effects: How SFX Became the Director's Lifeline." https://www.empireonline.com/movies/features/steven-spielberg-special-effects/. Accessed June 9, 2019.

page 25, line 14: Spielberg.

page 26, sidebar, line 7: "Steven Spielberg & Cast: The BFG Interview." https://www.movies4kids.co.uk/news/2016/07/21/steven-spielberg-cast-the-bfg-interview/. Accessed June 10, 2019.

page 27, line 6: Tom Shone. "Steven Spielberg: 'It's All About Making Kids Feel Like They Can Do Anything.'" https://www.theguardian.com/film/2016/jul/16/steven-spielberg-kids-can-do-anything-bfg. Accessed June 12, 2019.

page 29, line 5: ibid.

All internet sites appearing in back matter were available and accurate when this book was sent to press.

Printed in the United States of America.
PA99

TABLE OF CONTENTS

1 ▷ THE SHARK SINKS

Imagine a hot summer afternoon on a crowded beach. Kids are laughing and splashing in the ocean. Suddenly, a boy cries out. The water turns red. Shark attack! Everyone panics. Swimmers scream and race for shore. Then someone yells, "Cut!"

It was the summer of 1974. A young filmmaker named Steven Spielberg was directing his first big feature film, *Jaws*. An adventure at sea, the movie is about a great white shark eating swimmers alive.

When the movie opened the next year, millions of people flocked to their nearest theater. Audiences around the world were terrified. *Jaws* broke box office records. Steven became famous.

But during that 1974 summer, Steven wasn't famous yet. He was miserable.

Lights, Camera, Action!

There are several major players needed to make a movie. The movie's director works with a script, written by the movie's writer. He or she decides how to show and tell the story on-screen. Everyone who works on the movie, including the actors, photographers, and editors, answers to the director. Movie producers come up with and manage the money needed to pay for the film. Producers are often on the movie set. Executive producers help pay for the film but do not work on-set.

Jaws takes place in the fictional town of Amity, in New England. However, it was filmed in Martha's Vineyard, an island in Massachusetts.

There were so many problems during the making of *Jaws* that the cast and crew nicknamed the movie *"Flaws."* Everything was going wrong. Part of the reason was because Steven was trying something new. Before *Jaws*, directors didn't film movies in the ocean. But Steven insisted. He knew audiences would be more scared if they were fully **immersed** in the story.

However, making a movie at sea was much harder than he expected. "I was **naïve** about the ocean," he said later. "I was too young to know I was being foolhardy when I demanded that we shoot the film in the Atlantic Ocean and not in a North Hollywood tank." Soon, things were way behind schedule.

The ocean was as real as it could get. There was bad weather. One day Steven's boat sank, with cast, crew, and cameras on board. But the biggest nightmare was the star of the movie himself—the shark.

immerse—to be involved deeply in a particular activity or interest
naïve—showing a lack of experience, wisdom, or judgement

Steven couldn't cast a real shark in the movie. Great white sharks are too dangerous to train. And at the time, designing a computer-generated shark was impossible. So the movie studio built a giant mechanical shark. Steven named it Bruce, after his lawyer. On land, Bruce was scary. But his first day in the ocean, Bruce splashed, sputtered, and instantly sunk.

There were actually three Bruces built. Two rode on underwater sleds and could leap out of the water. The third was pulled by a boat when Bruce needed to swim.

DID YOU KNOW?

Steven was so angry at Bruce that he nicknamed him "the Great White Turd."

How could Steven tell a story about a shark without a shark? Then he got an idea. "What you *don't* see is generally scarier than what you *do* see," he said. Shooting underwater, he filmed swimmers from the shark's point of view. Shooting above water, he gave hints about something lurking below. In editing, he added suspenseful, terrifying music. The shark barely appears in the movie at all, but audiences were scared silly.

Steven had nightmares about *Jaws* for many years after. Two months of filming stretched into five. The original film budget of $3.5 million ballooned to $10 million.

Steven and Bruce, 1975. *Jaws* made more than $470 million at the theater. That's nearly $2 billion in today's money.

In the end, though, Steven was rewarded. Movie watchers spent hundreds of millions of dollars to see a movie with the tagline, "You'll never go in the water again." Jaws became the first summer blockbuster in history. It won three Academy Awards in 1976 and was nominated for Best Picture. "The success of that changed my life," Steven said. "Jaws was a free pass into my future."

"You'll Never Go in the Water Again"

The music in Jaws is as famous as the movie itself. "I think the **score** was clearly responsible for half of the success of that movie," Steven said. He and **composer** John Williams have worked together on nearly all of Steven's films. John doesn't compose any music until the film is nearly finished. Then he and Steven talk about where to put music and how it will help the story. "John Williams has been the single most significant contributor to my success as a filmmaker," Steven said.

composer—a person who writes songs or music
score—a musical composition written for a movie or theatrical production
tagline—catchy words or phrases used to advertise a movie

2

THE BUDDING FILMMAKER

Steven Allen Spielberg was born on December 18, 1946, in Cincinnati, Ohio. He was raised in a Jewish family. His mother, Leah, played piano, and his father, Arnold, was a computer engineer.

When Steven was 10 years old, he borrowed his father's movie camera and never gave it back. He filmed elaborate train wrecks with his toy train set. He shot horror movies starring—and terrifying—his three little sisters. He directed the action on family vacations. When he was a 12-year-old Boy Scout, he made a short Western movie. Casting his fellow Scouts in leading roles, Steven also created **special effects**. He used ketchup for blood and pillows for **stunt doubles**. The Scouts loved the film, and Steven loved their applause. He won a photography merit badge for his work and, best of all, made some friends.

Lights, Camera, Spielberg Family!

A flair for entertainment ran in the Spielberg family. Steven's great uncle, Boris, was an actor and a lion tamer in the circus. His grandfather, Fievel, sang, danced, and played guitar. And everyone in Steven's family loved stories. A Russian-Jewish **immigrant**, Fievel told Steven many tales about Jewish life in the old country.

Years later, Steven was the executive producer for *An American Tail*. The movie was an animated story about a mouse coming to America. Its star, Fievel Mousekewitz, was named after Steven's grandfather.

Steven and his father, Arnold, at the movie premiere of *The Land Before Time* in 1989.

immigrant—someone who comes from one country to live permanently in another country

special effect—an illusion created for movies or TV using special props, camera systems, computer graphics, and other methods

stunt double—a trained professional who performs dangerous or physically demanding stunts in place of an actor

But although making movies was fun and easy, making friends was harder. The Spielberg family moved often. Being the new kid—and often the only Jewish kid—was difficult for Steven. He wasn't good at sports and was often bullied. "I just was a lonely guy," he said later.

Over the years, many actors have praised Steven's knowledge of filmmaking.

Steven was happiest telling stories with his camera. His parents pitched in to help their talented son. Arnold found Steven a World War II airplane for one of his films. Leah made costumes for another movie. And when Steven was in high school, the family rented a movie theater in town to premiere his **sci-fi** film *Firelight*.

Steven's **amateur** films and creative special effects won attention and awards. In 1962, 15-year-old Steven won a film festival with his 40-minute film *Escape to Nowhere*. "I knew that this was going to be a career, not just a hobby," Steven said later.

Things on the big screen were coming together. But at home, Steven's parents were growing apart. In 1964, the family moved to California. Soon after, Leah and Arnold divorced. Unsettled and unhappy, Steven was even more determined to make movies. And now Hollywood was only a short drive away.

amateur—done by people who play for fun, not money
sci-fi—short for science fiction

One summer vacation, Steven talked his way into Universal Studios. He was hired in the studio's television department as an unpaid assistant. Once on the inside, he watched real filmmakers at work. He introduced himself to everyone and tried to learn everything possible. Even after school started in the fall, he kept going back to the studio.

Universal Studios was founded in 1912. It is the fourth oldest film studio in the world.

DID YOU KNOW?

In 1981, Steven helped start a production company called Amblin Entertainment.

A few years later, he met a producer at Universal who helped him make a short film called *Amblin'*. When Steven showed his work to studio executives, they offered him a seven-year directing contract. He was the youngest director ever hired for a long period of time with a major studio.

At age 22, Steven was on his way to movie greatness. But he would never forget his lonely childhood. His memories would play a big part in his future films.

Breaking In to the Movies

Steven's filmmaking talent was obvious even when he was in high school. But his grades weren't good enough to get him accepted into film school. He ended up enrolling at California State University, Long Beach. He "studied" filmmaking at Universal. He dropped out of college when the studio hired him. In 2002, he finally returned to Long Beach to complete his bachelor's degree in film.

3

ACTION AND ADVENTURE

Steven did some directing for TV shows and movies. Producers saw his talent and offered him the chance to direct Jaws.

After the ocean thriller, everyone wanted another Spielberg flick. But what kind of movie did he want to make? An intergalactic adventure? An earthbound thriller? A fantasy about a lonely little boy and a lost space alien who become best friends? Steven made all three and directed one hit after another.

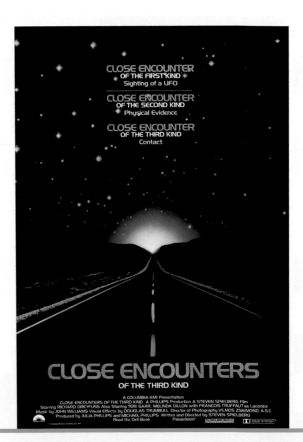

On the film's 30th anniversary, *Close Encounters of the Third Kind* was added to the National Film Registry. Films in the registry are chosen for being "culturally, historically, or aesthetically" significant.

Close Encounters

In the late 1940s, astronomer J. Allen Hynek began working for the government. He reviewed reports of UFO sightings. At first, he was skeptical. But he became a believer. In 1972, he published *The UFO Experience*. He can be seen briefly in Steven's movie.

According to Dr. Hynek, there are three kinds of encounters with aliens that one can experience. The first kind means you've seen a UFO. The second kind involves seeing something caused by a UFO, like mysterious lights or toys coming alive at night. Actually coming into contact with aliens or a UFO is a "close encounter of the third kind."

Close Encounters of the Third Kind came out in 1977, two years after *Jaws*. In the movie, a supernatural force takes over a small Indiana town. One man leaves his family to find out what's happening, only to face off against the scientists who are hiding the truth.

Using spectacular special effects, Steven made houses shake, toys come alive at night, and unidentified flying objects (UFOs) streak across a starlit sky. It was a big budget version of his high school film, *Firelight*, and it was a hit. Steven received his first nomination for Best Director.

In 1981, kids and grown-ups alike cheered for a fearless **archaeologist** named Indiana "Indy" Jones in *Raiders of the Lost Ark*. Set in 1936, Indy crosses continents to find a mysterious ancient treasure before the Nazis get to it first. He battles bad guys with swords, is nearly crushed by a rolling boulder, and comes face-to-face with 10,000 hissing snakes.

The very next year, Steven gave audiences another hero—this time, from outer space. *E.T. the Extra-Terrestrial* tells the story of a surprising friendship between a 10-year-old boy named Elliott and a space alien named E.T. Accidentally left on Earth after his spaceship flies home, E.T. hides in Elliott's backyard. Elliott is frightened when he first finds the strange-looking creature, but they quickly become best friends.

DID YOU KNOW?

Star Wars director George Lucas came up with the idea for *Raiders of the Lost Ark*. The movie won five Academy Awards and was nominated for four more, including Best Director. Steven directed three **sequels** between 1984 and 2008.

Fans weren't ready to say goodbye to the adventures of Indiana Jones. A fifth movie in the series was announced in late 2018.

archaeologist—someone who studies how people lived in the past
sequel—the next part of a story

E.T. is one of Steven's most famous movies and also one of his most personal. "I saw my childhood through this family and those young actors," Steven said. Elliott's parents are divorced, like Steven's. Elliott is a lonely little boy, like Steven was. "When I was a kid, I used to imagine strange creatures . . . and I'd wish that they'd come into my life and magically change it," Steven remembered.

Magically changing Elliott's life, E.T. heals Elliott's cut finger. He makes Elliott's bike fly. He and Elliott understand each other. When the little alien says, "E.T., phone home," Elliott knows he must help his friend go home, even though it means saying goodbye forever.

E.T. sold more than 120 million tickets during its first theatrical release. It is still one of the highest-grossing movies of all time.

"When I did the goodbye scene, I couldn't stop crying," said Henry Thomas, the actor who played Elliott. "He was real to me."

DID YOU KNOW?

E.T. won four Academy Awards and, for the third time, Steven was nominated for Best Director. At one film festival, the audience stood and applauded for nearly half an hour.

Who Was E.T.?

Steven and his special effects team made the lovable alien come to life in several different ways. Some scenes featured an **animatronic** E.T. puppet. Others involved actors wearing costumes. To shoot close-ups of E.T.'s hands, Steven hired a mime who wore special gloves. The little alien's face was based on paintings and photos of famous people, including Albert Einstein.

animatronic—made lifelike by using a special technique

4 ▶ BEST DIRECTOR

As Steven got older, he wanted to tackle more serious subjects. In the 1980s, he directed *The Color Purple* and *Empire of the Sun*. Both films, realistic stories about tragedy and loss, prepared Steven to make one of his greatest films ever—*Schindler's List*.

Schindler's List is a true story. It is about a German businessman named Oskar Schindler who saved the lives of more than 1,000 Polish Jews during the **Holocaust**. Steven read the book in the early 1980s. But he didn't feel ready to make the movie for another ten years.

The subject was painful. Growing up, Steven knew that his own Polish and Ukrainian relatives were among the 6 million Jews killed in the Holocaust. But as the target of childhood bullies himself, Steven often didn't like being Jewish. "I was always aware I stood out because of my Jewishness," he said. "All I wanted to do was fit in."

From Fantasy to Reality

After working with the child actors on *E.T.*, Steven was ready to be a dad himself. He and his first wife, actress Amy Irving, had a son in 1985. Steven and his second wife, Kate Capshaw, have a blended family of seven children.

Steven's feelings changed as he matured, and especially after he had children himself. "I wanted them to be raised as Jews," Steven said. He also wanted them to understand their history. In 1993, Steven was finally ready to make *Schindler's List*. He brought his whole family with him to the movie set.

Steven and actor Liam Neeson shooting *Schindler's List* in 1993. The movie was shot in black and white.

Holocaust—the mass murder during World War II of millions of Jews, as well as Romani, disabled people, gay people, and political and religious leaders

Steven shot *Schindler's List* exactly where the real events had taken place during the Holocaust. Recreating some of those scenes was difficult for cast and crew. To help Steven cope, comedian Robin Williams called every week to tell him jokes.

Yet unbelievably, after shooting *Schindler's List* all day, Steven worked on the special effects for his next movie at night. *Jurassic Park* is about science gone wrong. Scientists bring dinosaurs back to life to fill a theme park. But the creatures break free, with terrifying results.

Steven and movie producer Kathleen Kennedy on the set of *Jurassic Park*.

Twenty years after *Jaws*, technology had come a long way. The *Jurassic Park* dinosaurs were created with a combination of animatronic and robotic puppets and computer-generated imagery (CGI). They moved smoothly and ran like the wind. The effects were jaw-dropping. "I could not believe my eyes," Steven said.

Both *Jurassic Park* and *Schindler's List* were released in 1993. Each won many awards. After three Best Director nominations, Steven finally took home the Academy Award for *Schindler's List*. But recalling his childhood shame about being Jewish, he knew he had won something even bigger. "The experience of making *Schindler's List*," he said, "made me so proud to be a Jew."

DID YOU KNOW?

In 1999, Steven won his second Best Director Academy Award for another war film, *Saving Private Ryan*.

After *Schindler's List*, Steven co-founded his own film studio called DreamWorks. He opened a restaurant called Dive. And he continued to pick stories he wanted to tell. Over the next 20 years, Steven made movies about President Abraham Lincoln, artificial intelligence, slavery, soldiers, and spies. Then in 2016, Steven directed *The BFG*. He wanted to bring author Roald Dahl's Big Friendly Giant to life.

Advanced Technology

Steven and his team created the computer-animated giants in *The BFG* with motion capture technology. This complicated technique records the movements of a real person, then translates the digital information into computer animation. "With the digital revolution today, there is no limit to anyone's imagination," Steven said. "You can literally put anything on the screen."

The *BFG* is about a lonely giant and an orphan named Sophie. The two become good friends. Together, they defeat a gang of giant bullies. Considering his own painful childhood, *The BFG* is the kind of story Steven has always loved to tell. "It's all about making kids feel like they can do anything," he said. "That nothing's impossible."

DID YOU KNOW?

Both *The BFG and E.T.* were about lonely children who find unusual and wonderful friendships. Steven's good friend Melissa Mathison wrote the screenplays for both movies.

Steven and composer John Williams at the movie premiere for *The BFG*.

When he was a little boy, Steven loved to listen to his grandfather's stories. Then he used a camera to tell his own tales. Over the past five decades, he has directed and produced dozens of feature films. He has won top honors from the movie industry, universities, and government leaders. He has received the Presidential Medal of Freedom and a star on the Hollywood Walk of Fame. He even carried the flag during opening ceremonies of the 2002 Winter Olympics.

Steven was given a star at Hollywood Boulevard on January 10, 2003.

Steven Spielberg is one of the most popular filmmakers in movie history. But at night, now he thrills a much smaller audience. Just like his grandfather, he tells bedtime stories to his own grandchildren. "I just love doing it," Steven said. "They're all stories of . . . being magical . . . or your best friend being a tyrannosaurus rex. . . . I look forward to it, the same way I look forward to making the next movie."

Shoah Foundation

Steven refused to take a salary for directing *Schindler's List*. He had spoken to many Holocaust survivors about their experiences, and he didn't want to profit off their history. Instead, he used the money to found the Shoah Foundation Institute for Visual History and Education. Shoah is the Hebrew word for "Holocaust." The foundation has recorded the stories of nearly 55,000 Holocaust survivors in 65 countries, in 43 languages.

GLOSSARY

amateur (AM-uh-chur)—done by people who play for fun, not money

animatronic (an-uh-muh-TRAHN-ik)—made lifelike by using a special technique

archaeologist (ar-kee-AH-luh-jist)—someone who studies how people lived in the past

composer (kom-POH-zuhr)—a person who writes songs or music

extra-terrestrial (ek-struh-tuh-RESS-tree-uhl)—a life-form that comes from outer space; extraterrestrial means "outside of Earth"

Holocaust (HAH-luh-khost)—the mass murder during World War II of millions of Jews, as well as Romani, disabled people, gay people, and political and religious leaders

immerse (ih-MURS)—to be involved deeply in a particular activity or interest

immigrant (IM-uh-gruhnt)—someone who comes from one country to live permanently in another country

naïve (ni-EEV)—showing a lack of experience, wisdom, or judgement

sci-fi (SYE-FYE)—short for science fiction; a story about life in the future or on another planet

score (SKOR)—a musical composition written for a movie or theatrical production

sequel (SEE-kwuhl)—the next part of a story

special effect (SPESH-uhl uh-FEKTS)—illusion created for movies or TV using special props, camera systems, computer graphics, and other methods

stunt double (STUHNT DUH-buhl)—a trained professional who performs dangerous or physically demanding stunts in place of an actor

tagline (TAHG-line)—catchy words or phrases used to advertise a movie

READ MORE

Green, Sara. *Visual Effects.* Minneapolis: Bellwether Media, 2020.

Higgins, Nadia. *Making a Movie.* Mankato, MN: Amicus/Amicus Ink, 2019.

Troupe, Thomas Kingsley. *Shoot Epic Short Documentaries: 4D An Augmented Reading Experience.* North Mankato, MN: Capstone Press, 2020.

INTERNET SITES

Film Future. Filmmaking for Kids
http://www.filmmakingforkids.com/

Hollywood Walk of Fame
https://www.walkoffame.com/

Kiddle: Steven Spielberg Facts for Kids
https://kids.kiddle.co/Steven_Spielberg

CRITICAL THINKING QUESTIONS

1. How have Steven's family and life experiences impacted the kinds of movies he makes?

2. Steven uses his vision as a filmmaker to bring stories to life. What is your favorite story? Draw a movie poster, then write a tagline and summary of the plot for it.

3. Think of a story you have heard recently. It may be a book, a newspaper article, or even a story you heard from a friend. Would it make a good movie? Why or why not?

INDEX